BRITISH RAILWAY MAPS
OF YESTERYEAR

LONDON

IAN ALLAN LTD

GREAT NORTHERN RAILWAY

TIME TABLE

No. 275

EXPRESS ROUTE

Between **LONDON** (King's Cross)

NOTTINGHAM	LEEDS	SCARBORO'
SHEFFIELD	BRADFORD	NEWCASTLE
MANCHESTER	HULL	EDINBURGH
GRIMSBY	YORK	GLASGOW

and all **SCOTLAND**

OCT. 1st, 1912, to JUNE 30th, 1913.

Contents

INDEX TO MAPS

First published 1991

ISBN 0 7110 2019 1

Published by Ian Allan Ltd, Shepperton, Surrey; and phototypeset and printed by Ian Allan Printing Ltd at their works at Coombelands in Runnymede, England

This collection of maps has been culled from the pre-Grouping and Grouped Railways' Timetables from the archives of the National Railway Museum, York and of Ian Allan. It is interspersed by interesting cover illustrations and advertisement pages to reflect the atmosphere of yesteryear railways.

Railway Maps of Yesteryear

A study of railway cartography shows that during the last hundred years fairly accurately geographical maps of railway systems have degenerated — and I use the word advisedly — into diagrammatic representations of passenger train services. Currently, indeed, for some years the railway authorities have not produced anything remotely like a system map of realistic proportions or accurately defined junctions, which so often appear as some sort of cross roads, giving no indication of the actual layout.

This was unheard of in days of yore when every company claimed cartographically at least twice as much territory as it actually owned or served but always clearly defined its junctions, avoiding lines, spurs and in some cases even extended loops. In the pages which follow this is graphically set out, never more so than in the London area where practically every railway line was claimed as its own by every company!

We have secured timetable maps for each of the major pre-grouping companies and these mostly pre-date the 1914-18 war whilst those in respect of the Big Four were published just before the Second World War. Included are some of the magnificently illustrated timetable front covers which really are works of art in their own right, whilst some of the contemporary advertisements evince a reflection of those spacious days when one could spend the night in a luxury hotel, have dinner and still have ample change from a sovereign.

Maps played a big part in the general publicity of the early railways when no doubt Joe Public was either better educated in their use or had more time to study them and as can be seen from the LB&SCR's advertisement for "luggage-in-advance", the opportunity was seized to publish a railway map of the entire London area including stations underground whence no "PLA" could ever have been delivered. Maps and public relations were virtually inseparably inter-twined.

I have had a personal love of maps as far back as I can remember and it has, therefore, given me the greatest pleasure to plunder my own collection and to work with the National Railway Museum at York to whom I express my appreciation of their unstinted co-operation to produce this compilation of maps as a tribute to the artists of the past who produced these fascinating if slightly fictional representations of their companies' territory.

IA

The N.R.M.

The National Railway Museum Library & Archive is one of Britain's major reference sources for the study of railway history. The National Railway Museum has, since its opening in 1975, built up important collections of books, maps, archives and pictures which detail the historical and technical development of locomotives and rolling stock and reflect the growth of railway services in the United Kingdom.

The Collections

The *Printed Book* Collection contains most of the important works on railway development in Britain and includes some titles on overseas railways, particularly in the USA, France and Germany.

The *Periodical Collection* of over 500 titles, includes transactions of professional institutions such as the Institution of Locomotive Engineers, journals concerning the financial and technical aspects of the railway industry, such as Hearapath's Railway Magazine which dates from 1835, journals of railway study societies and magazines published for the railway enthusiast.

The *Timetable* Collection contains both working and public timetables from the 1840s to the present day. Bradshaw, the father of railway timetables, is well represented with copies from 1840 to 1961. The Midland weekly notices running from 1886 to 1922 give a detailed picture of the daily operation of Britain's third largest railway. Also represented are a range of timetables from all the major pre-nationalisation railway companies and after 1948 from British Rail.

Government Publications include the Board of Trade Railway Returns from 1858 to 1922 which contain a wealth of statistical information including the numbers and classes of passengers carried, the totals of locomotives, carriages and wagons in stock at the end of the year and the nature and quantity of goods carried by each railway company. The series is continued after 1922 with the Ministry of Transport Statistics, the British Transport Commission Report and Accounts and the British Railways Board Report and Accounts. The library also has copies of the official railway accident reports from 1855 and a series of Railway Clearing House publications including handbooks, regulations, maps and junction diagram books.

The Photograph Collection contains around ¾ million negatives and over 100 different collections. The negatives date from 1866 to the present day and range in format from 35mm film to 18" x 16" glass plates. The photographs were taken by the larger railway companies for official record purposes and by enthusiastic amateurs. The diverse topics covered by the railway photographers reflect the once considerable diversity of railway operations. Many negatives especially of locomotives and rolling stock are strictly formal in nature, but others reflect the working and social conditions of the railways at the time. A selection of reference prints can be consulted in the Reading Room.

The Archive Collections consist largely of technical material concerning the development of locomotives and rolling stock and includes specifications, reports, correspondence and drawings. Copies of technical drawings and track plans are available from the microfilmed collection which can be consulted in the Reading Room. Catalogues are available on request. Telephone (0904) 621261 ext 236.

The Pictorial Collection contains paintings, prints and engravings illustrating, in some detail, the growth of the railway industry from 1825 onwards. Of particular interest are the wash drawings of J. C. Bourne of the London & Birmingham Railway and paintings by Spencer Gore, Stanhope Forbes, Edna Lumb and other well known artists. The pictorial collection is rich in works depicting the impact of the railways on the landscape and on people's lives and contains a fine series of original railway poster art work. Photographic reference prints of the collection can be consulted in the Library Reading Room.

The Poster, Notices and Handbills Collection contains several thousand items from the early nineteenth century to the present day with particularly good coverage for the years between the First and Second World Wars. The posters capture various aspects of British life and work from holiday making to golf, track laying to signalling, refreshment cars to boat trains. Reference prints of the collection can be consulted in the Library Reading Room.

The Sound Archive contains a growing number of audio cassettes of interviews with railway employees from Sir William Stanier, Chief Mechanical Engineer of the London, Midland and Scottish Railway to signalmen and engine drivers. The cassettes can be heard in the Library Reading Room using the tape deck and headphones provided.

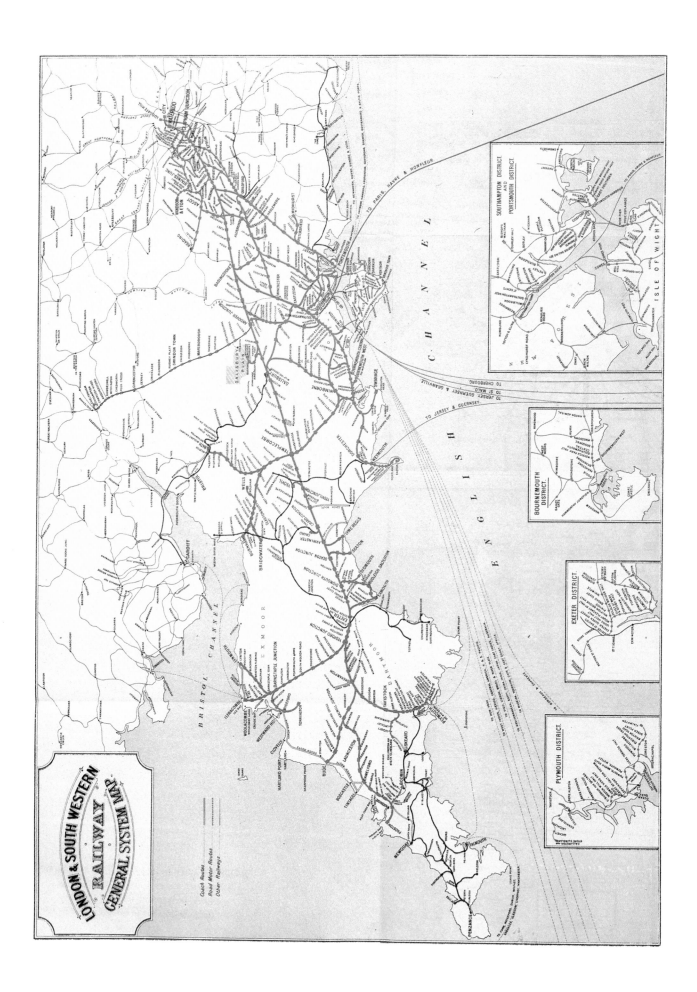

LONDON & SOUTH WESTERN RAILWAY
GENERAL SYSTEM MAP

Coach Routes
Road Motor Routes
Other Railways

SOUTHAMPTON DISTRICT. AND PORTSMOUTH DISTRICT.

BOURNEMOUTH DISTRICT.

EXETER DISTRICT.

PLYMOUTH DISTRICT.

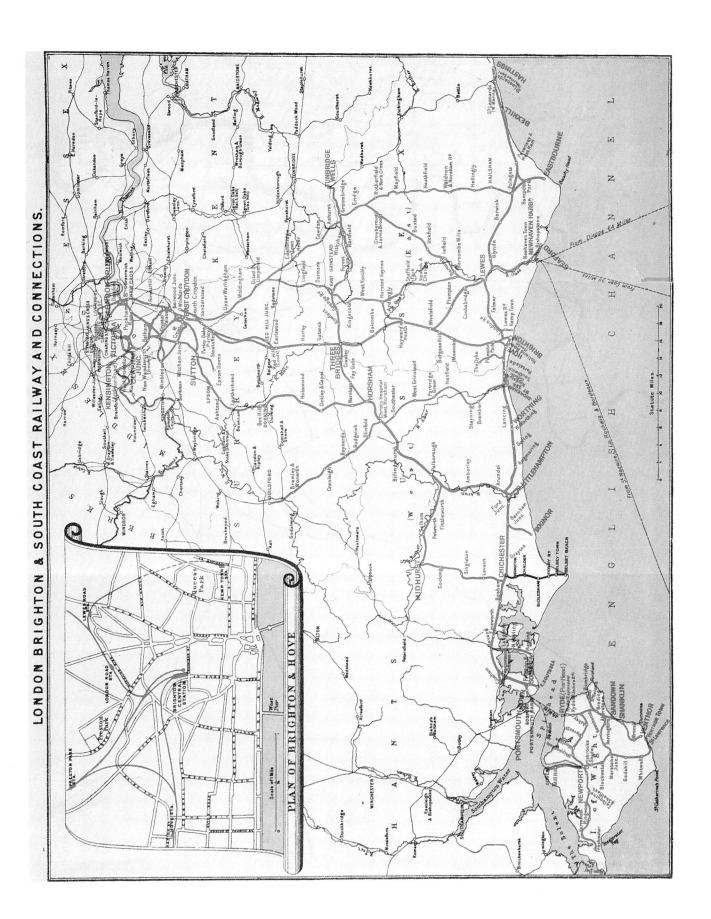

LONDON BRIGHTON & SOUTH COAST RAILWAY AND CONNECTIONS.

PLAN OF BRIGHTON & HOVE

7

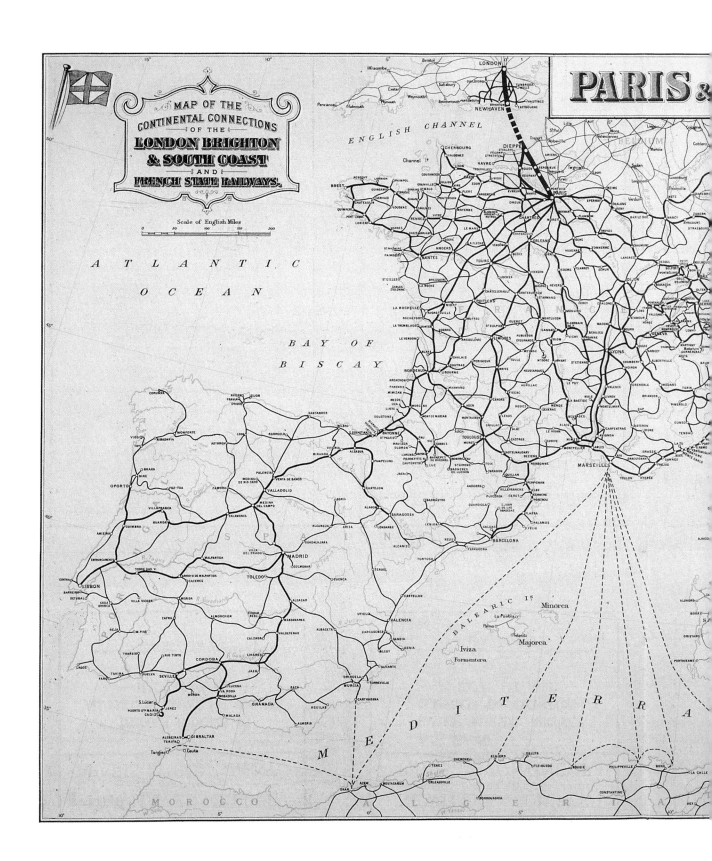

POLAND

CZECHO SLOVAKIA

AUSTRIA

HUNGARY

VIENNA

BUDAPEST

NUNBERG

MUNICH

SALZBURG

TRIESTE

VENICE

FIUME

JUGO SLAVIA

ROUMANIA

BUCHAREST

BULGARIA

SOFIA

ROME

NAPLES

ADRIATIC SEA

BRINDISI

BLACK SEA

CONSTANTINOPLE

GREECE

SALONICA

ATHENS

ASIA MINOR

SICILY

PALERMO

MESSINA

CATANIA

SYRACUSE

To Malta

From London and Dieppe

PARIS

ST LAZARE

VERSAILLES

9

LONDON, BRIGHTON & SOUTH COAST RAILWAY. Metropolitan and Suburban Lines and Connections.

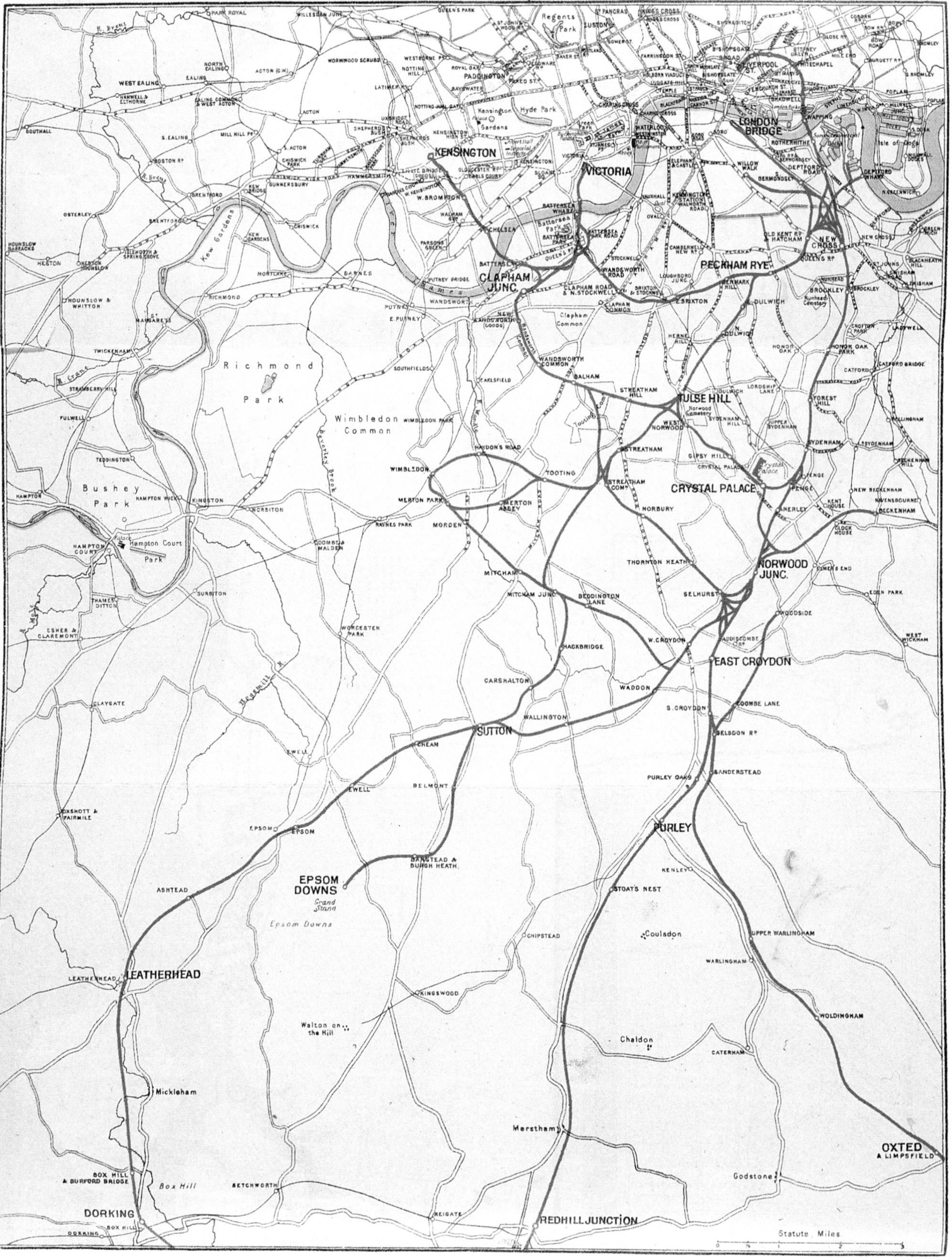

JUNE 7th to SEPTEMBER 30th, 1914, inclusive

THE SOUTH EASTERN AND CHATHAM RAILWAY COMPANIES
MANAGING COMMITTEE

SOUTH EASTERN AND CHATHAM RAILWAY

Time Tables

LONDON AND PARIS UNDER 7 HOURS

LONDON STATIONS

CHARING CROSS | VICTORIA
CANNON STREET | HOLBORN
LONDON BRIDGE | ST. PAUL'S

FRANCIS H. DENT,
General Manager.

McCorquodale & Co. Ltd., London.

PRICE TWOPENCE.

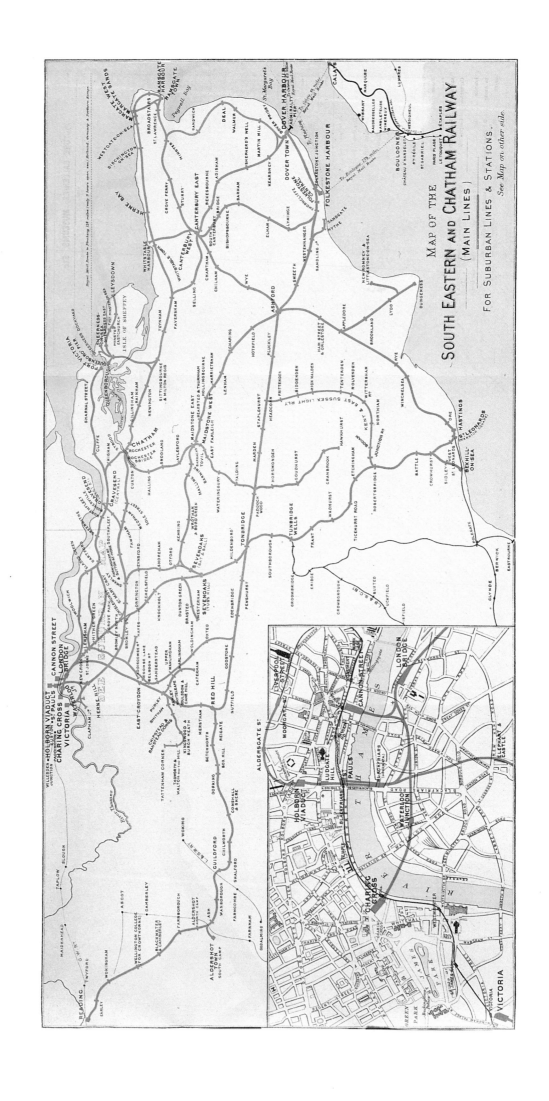

MAP OF THE

SOUTH EASTERN AND CHATHAM RAILWAY
(MAIN LINES)

For SUBURBAN LINES & STATIONS,

See Map on other side.

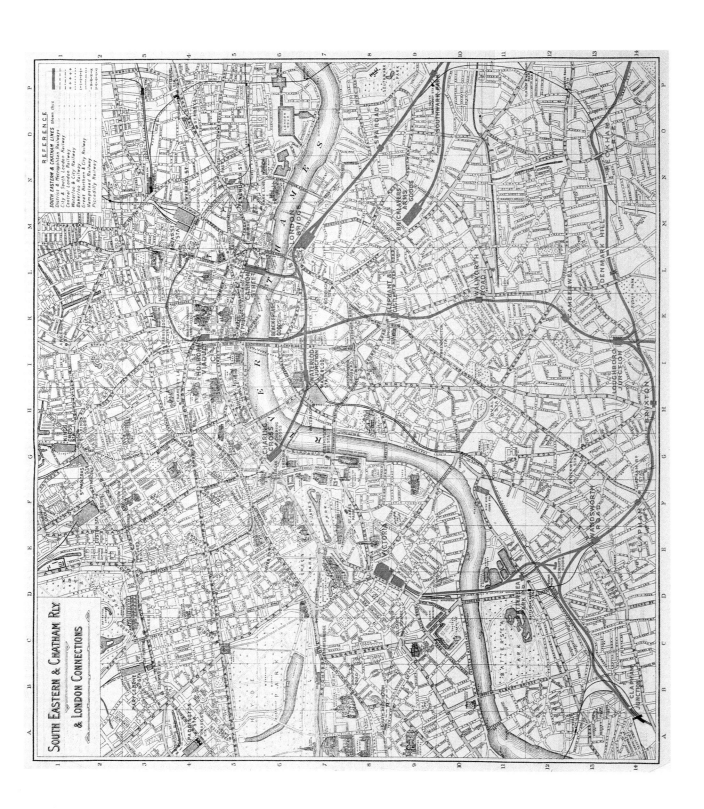

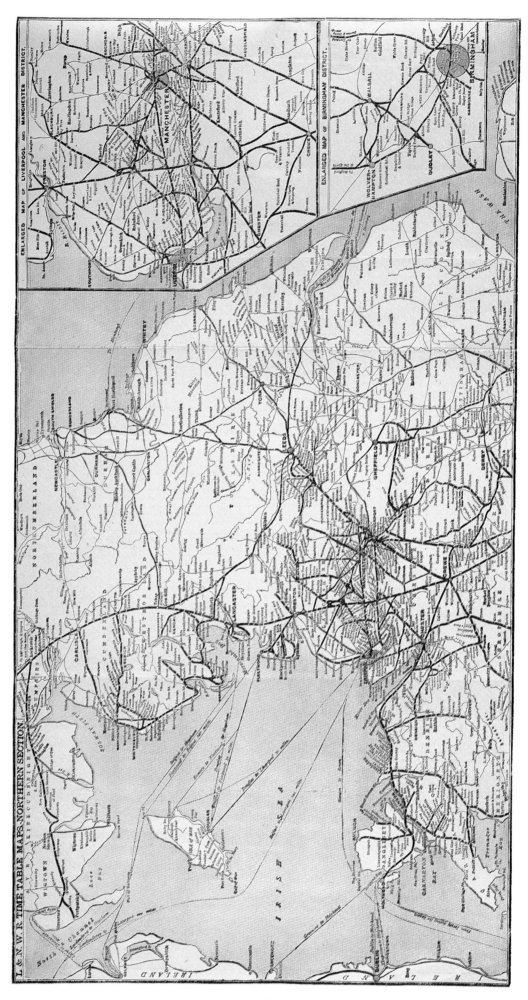

14

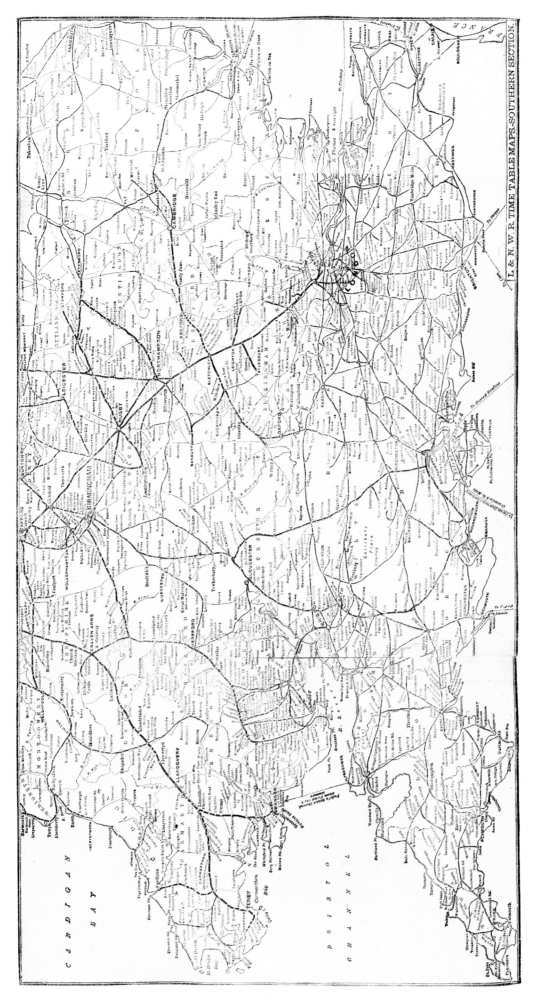

L. & N. W. R. TIME TABLE MAPS. SOUTHERN SECTION.

15

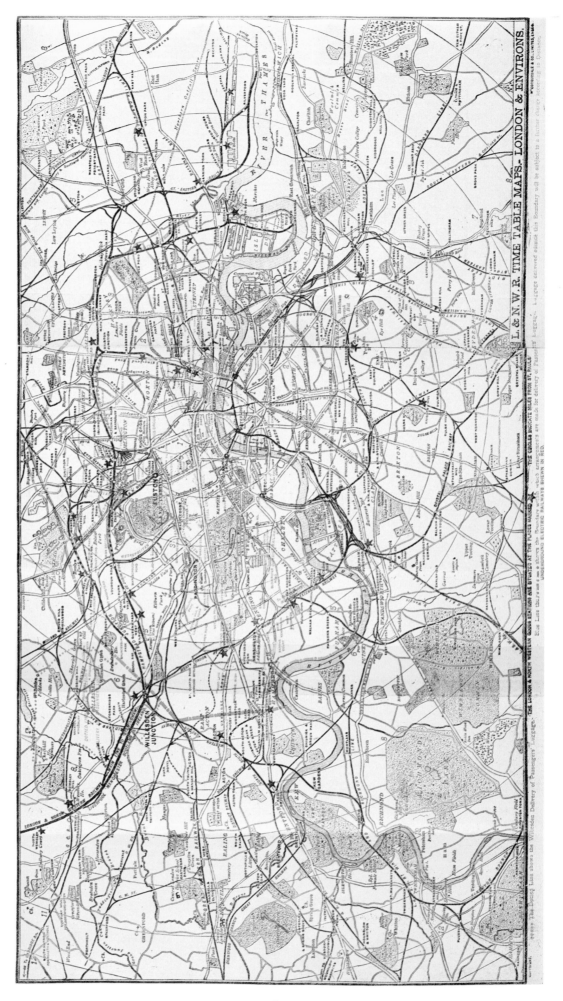

L. & N. W. R. TIME TABLE MAPS.— LONDON & ENVIRONS.

16

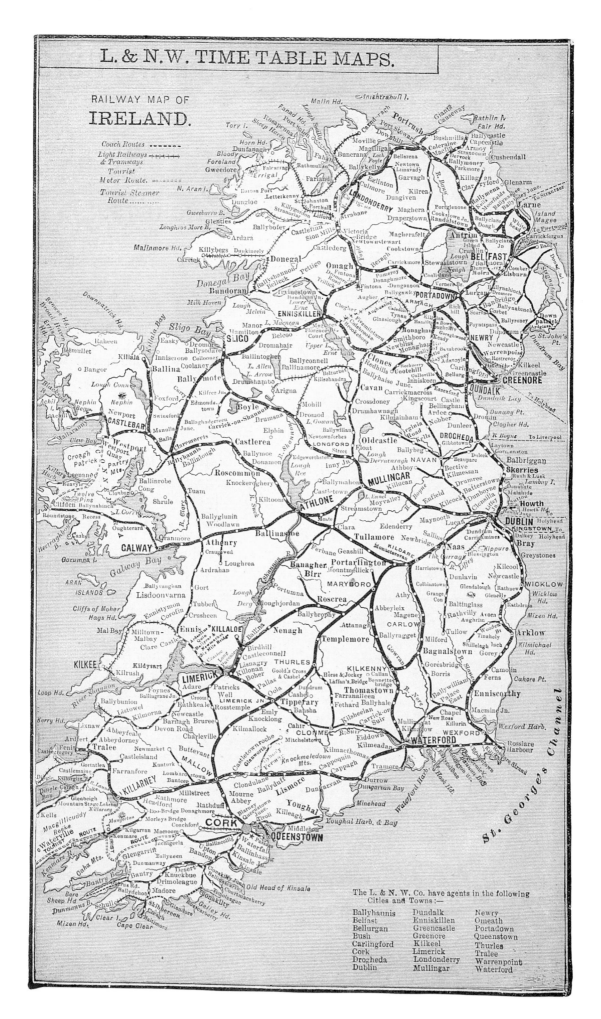

RAILWAY MAP OF
IRELAND.

Coach Routes --------
Light Railways
& Tramways ++++++++
Tourist
Motor Route. ========
Tourist Steamer
Route ....

The L. & N. W. Co. have agents in the following
Cities and Towns :—

Ballyhaunis	Dundalk	Newry
Belfast	Enniskillen	Omeath
Bellurgan	Greencastle	Portadown
Bush	Greenore	Queenstown
Carlingford	Kilkeel	Thurles
Cork	Limerick	Tralee
Drogheda	Londonderry	Warrenpoint
Dublin	Mullingar	Waterford

LANCASHIRE & YORKSHIRE
RAILWAY,
and its Connections.

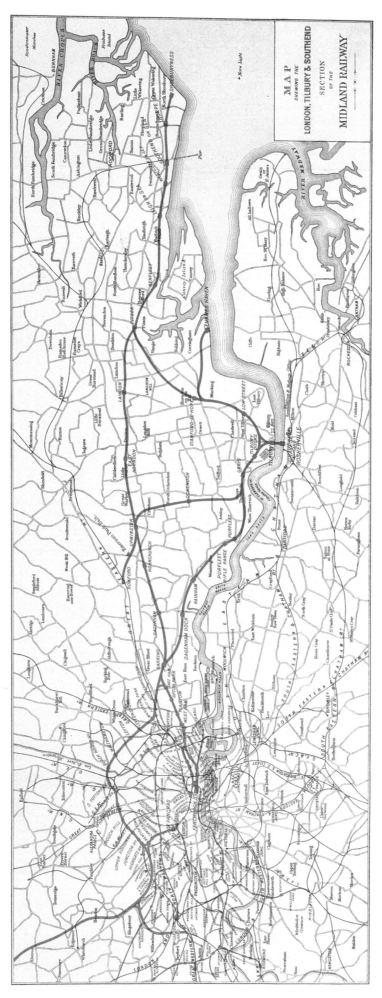

MAP
SHEWING THE
LONDON, TILBURY & SOUTHEND
SECTION
OF THE
MIDLAND RAILWAY

19

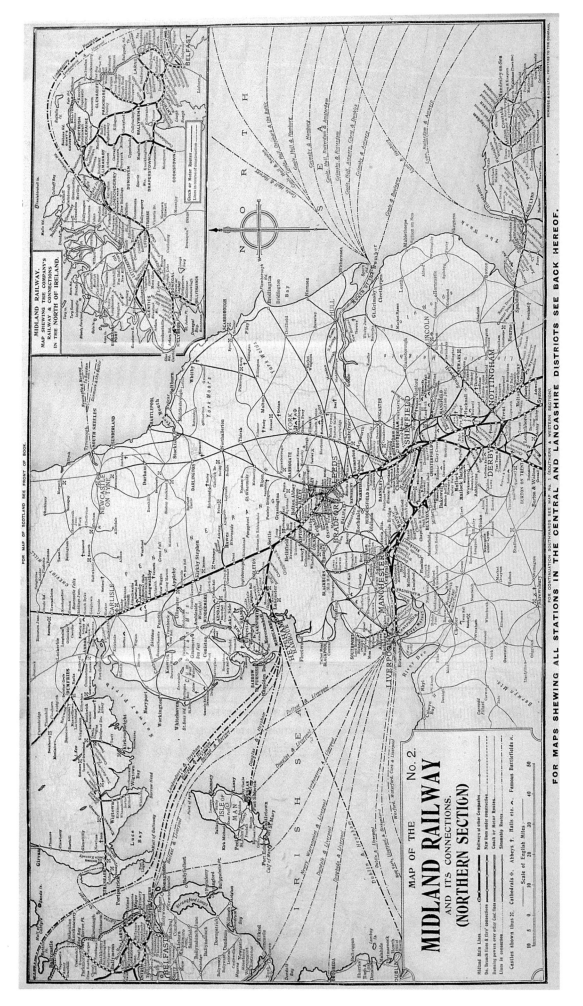

MAP OF THE No. 2.
MIDLAND RAILWAY
AND ITS CONNECTIONS.
(NORTHERN SECTION)

Midland Main Lines
Do. Branch lines & thro' connections
Running powers over other Coal lines
Lines in connection

Castles shown thus ☒.   Abbeys ⴕ.   Halls etc. ⋏.   Famous Battlefields ✕.

Scale of English Miles.
10 5 0   10   20   30   40   50

MIDLAND RAILWAY.
MAP SHEWING THE COMPANY'S
RAILWAY & CONNECTIONS
IN THE NORTH OF IRELAND.

Coach or Motor Routes
Lines in course of construction

FOR MAP OF SCOTLAND SEE FRONT OF BOOK.

FOR CONTINUATION SOUTHWARDS SEE MAP No. 1 (SOUTHERN & WESTERN SECTION)

FOR MAPS SHEWING ALL STATIONS IN THE CENTRAL AND LANCASHIRE DISTRICTS SEE BACK HEREOF.

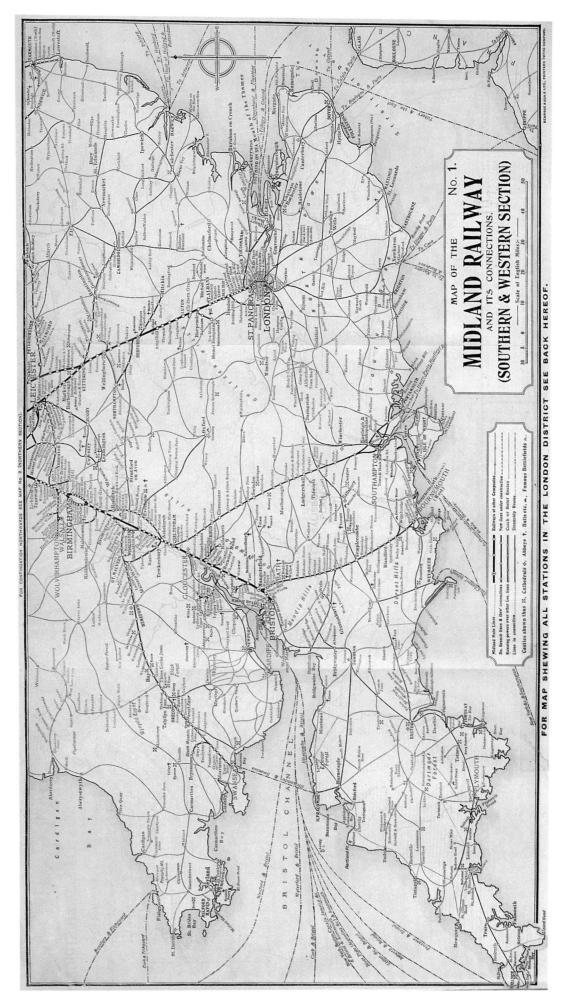

MAP OF THE No. 1.

MIDLAND RAILWAY
AND ITS CONNECTIONS.
(SOUTHERN & WESTERN SECTION)

Scale of English Miles:—

FOR MAP SHEWING ALL STATIONS IN THE LONDON DISTRICT SEE BACK HEREOF.

ONE PENNY.
FURNESS
RAILWAY
WINDERMERE
THE Tourist's Ideal Resort.
THROUGH CARRIAGES BETWEEN LONDON, LIVERPOOL, MANCHESTER, LEEDS, BRADFORD AND THE FURNESS LINE.
TIME TABLES
BARROW IN FURNESS.
OCTOBER 1ST, 1915,
UNTIL FURTHER NOTICE.
ALFRED ASLETT.
BARROW PRINTING CO., LTD., CROWN WORKS, LAWSON STREET.

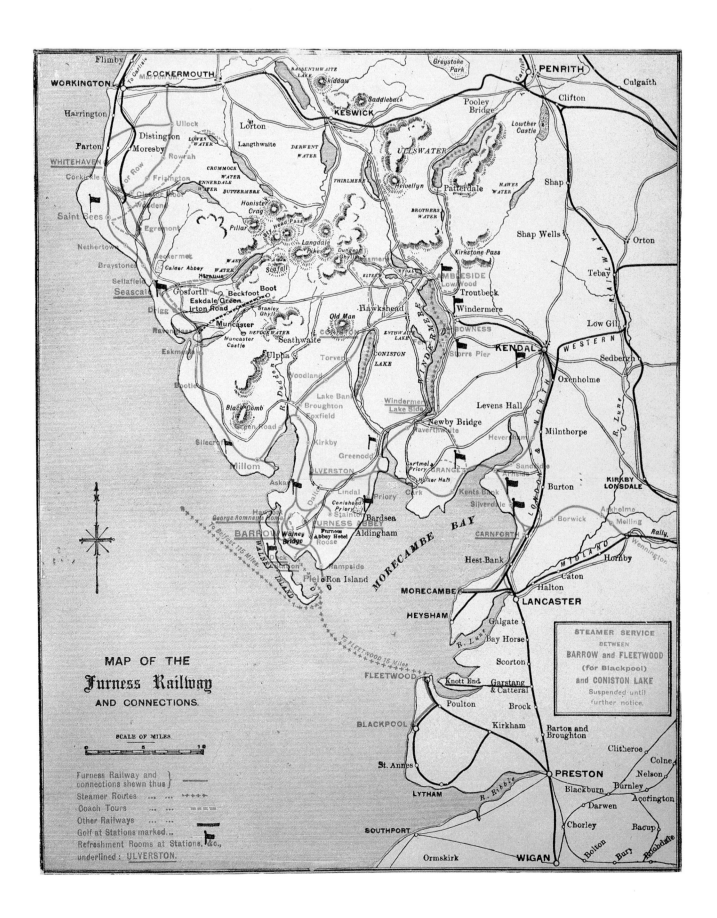

MAP OF THE
Furness Railway
AND CONNECTIONS.

SCALE OF MILES

Furness Railway and connections shewn thus
Steamer Routes ... ...
Coach Tours ... ...
Other Railways ... ...
Golf at Stations marked...
Refreshment Rooms at Stations, &c.,
underlined : ULVERSTON.

STEAMER SERVICE
BETWEEN
BARROW and FLEETWOOD
(for Blackpool)
and CONISTON LAKE
Suspended until
further notice.

23

GREAT CENTRAL RAILWAY & ITS CONNECTIONS.

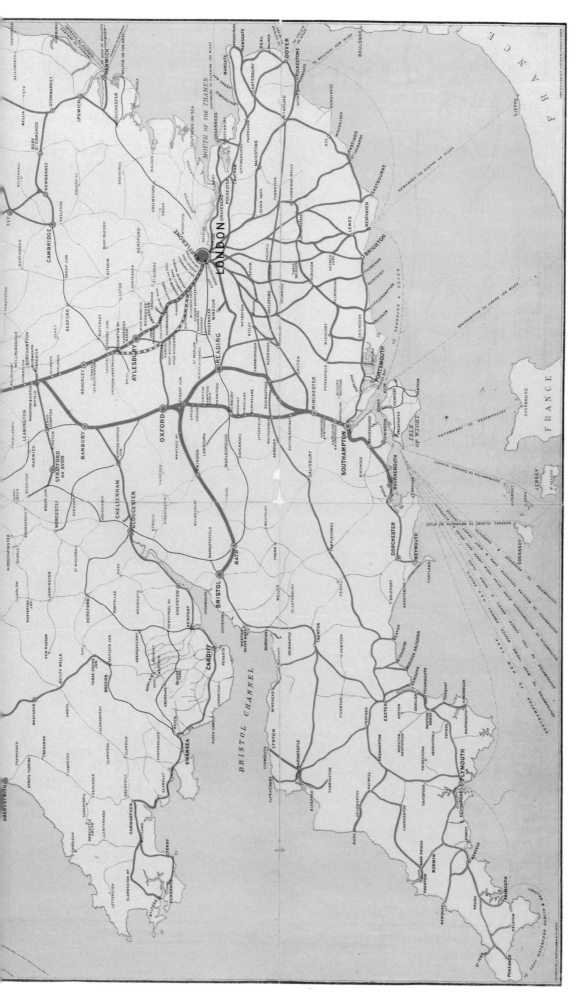

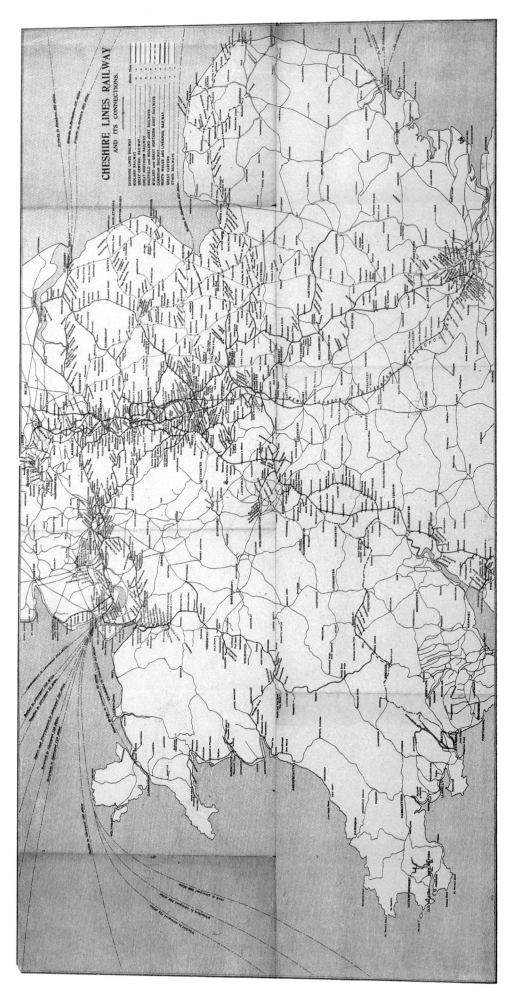

CHESHIRE LINES RAILWAY
AND ITS CONNECTIONS.

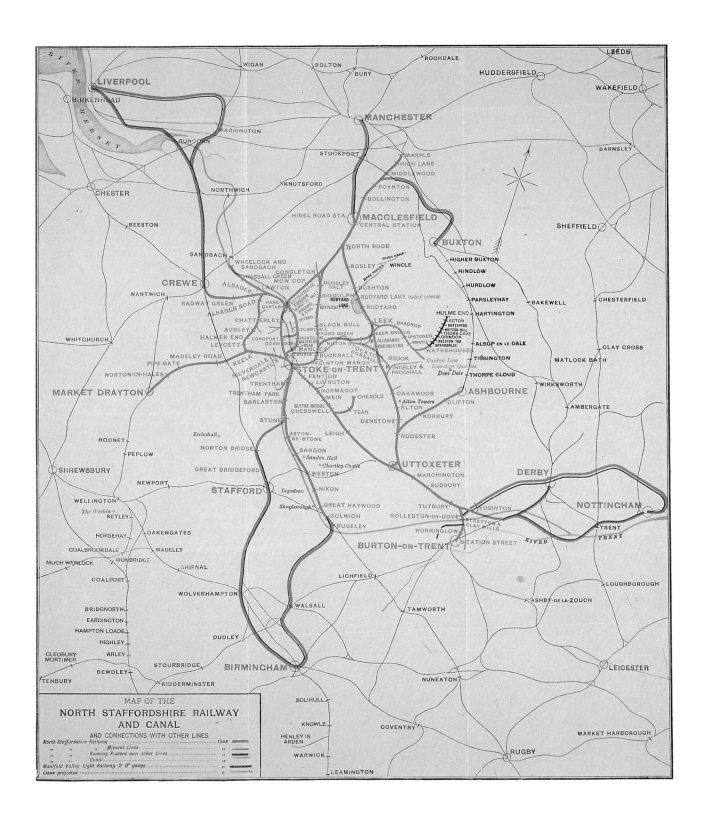

MAP OF THE
NORTH STAFFORDSHIRE RAILWAY
AND CANAL
AND CONNECTIONS WITH OTHER LINES

North Staffordshire Railway	....	thus	
"	" Mineral Lines	"	
"	" Running Powers over other Lines	"	
"	" Canal	"	
Manifold Valley Light Railway 2' 6" gauge	"	
Lines projected	....	"	

27

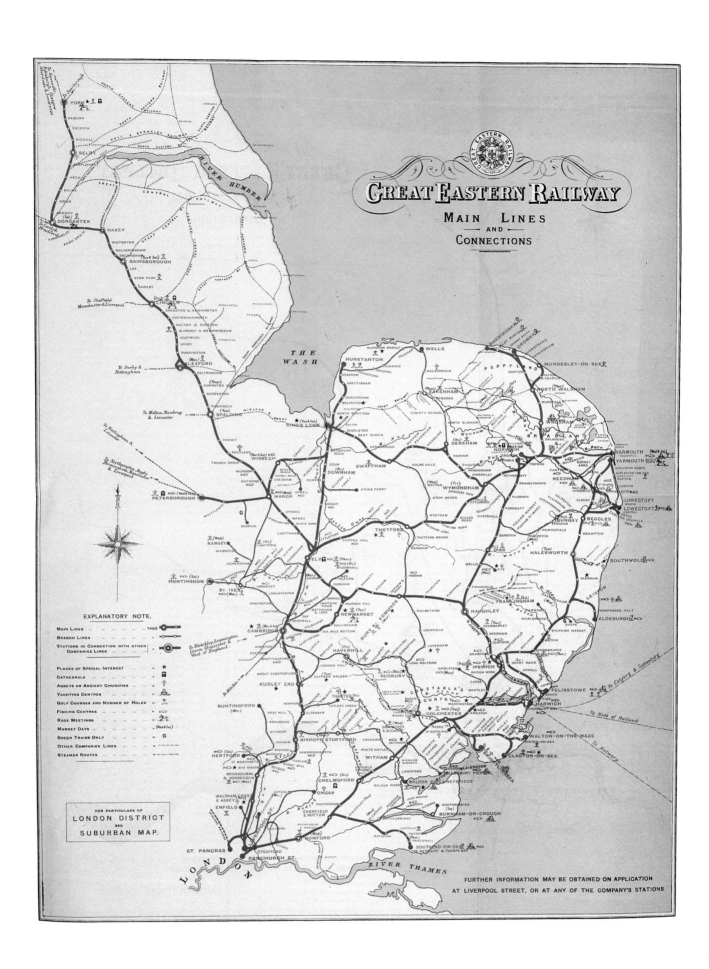

GREAT EASTERN RAILWAY
MAIN LINES
AND
CONNECTIONS

EXPLANATORY NOTE.

MAIN LINES .... THUS
BRANCH LINES ....
STATIONS IN CONNECTION WITH OTHER
COMPANIES LINES ....

PLACES OF SPECIAL INTEREST .... ★
CATHEDRALS ....
ABBEYS OR ANCIENT CHURCHES ....
YACHTING CENTRES ....
GOLF COURSES AND NUMBER OF HOLES ....
FISHING CENTRES ....
RACE MEETINGS ....
MARKET DAYS .... (Wed & Sat)
GOODS TRAINS ONLY .... G
OTHER COMPANIES LINES ....
STEAMER ROUTES ....

FOR PARTICULARS OF
LONDON DISTRICT
SEE
SUBURBAN MAP.

FURTHER INFORMATION MAY BE OBTAINED ON APPLICATION
AT LIVERPOOL STREET, OR AT ANY OF THE COMPANY'S STATIONS

EAST COAST ROUTE

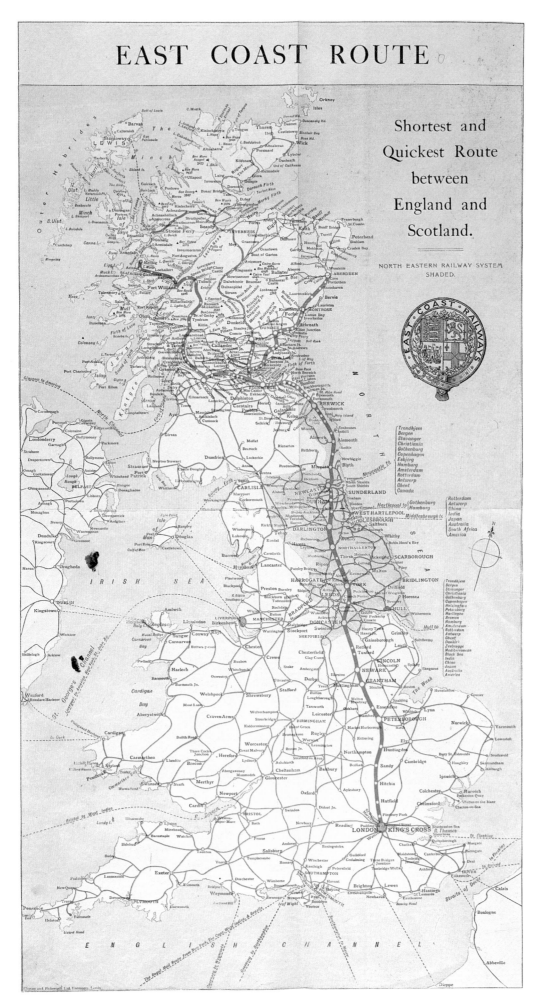

Shortest and
Quickest Route
between
England and
Scotland.

NORTH EASTERN RAILWAY SYSTEM
SHADED.

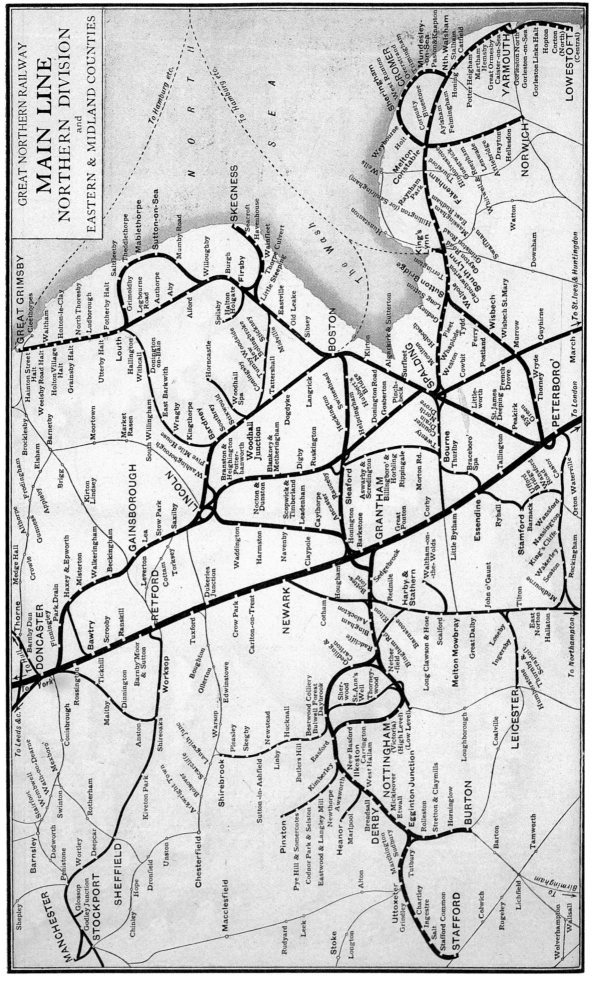

GREAT NORTHERN RAILWAY
MAIN LINE
NORTHERN DIVISION
and
EASTERN & MIDLAND COUNTIES

30

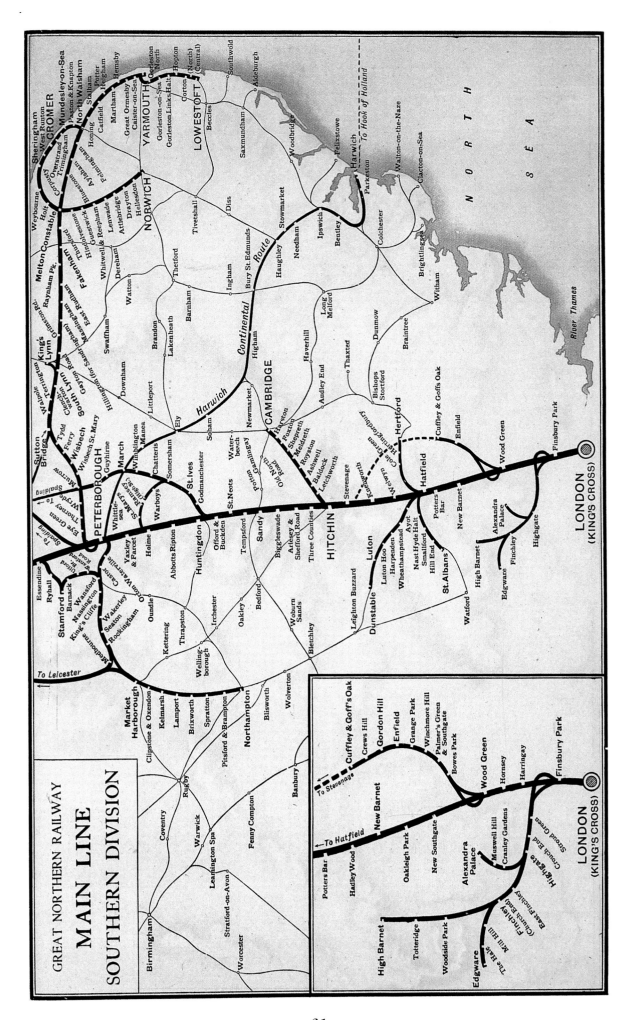

GREAT NORTHERN RAILWAY

MAIN LINE
SOUTHERN DIVISION

31

GREAT NORTHERN RAILWAY. — MAP OF LONDON AND SUBURBS.

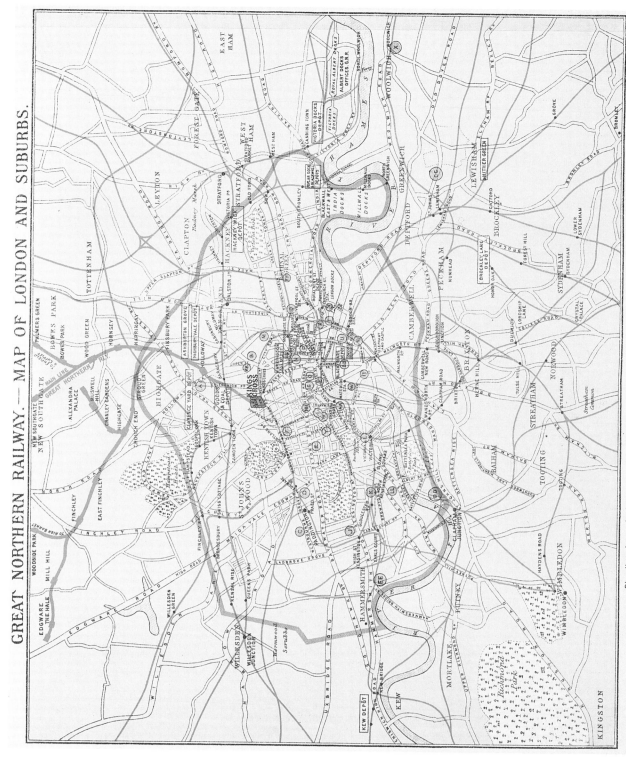

Blue line shows the boundary within which arrangements are made for delivery of passengers' luggage.

Luggage is delivered from all Great Northern Suburban Stations. Luggage delivered outside the boundary will be subject to a further charge according to distance.

G.N.R. YORKSHIRE AND LANCASHIRE DISTRICT CONNECTIONS.

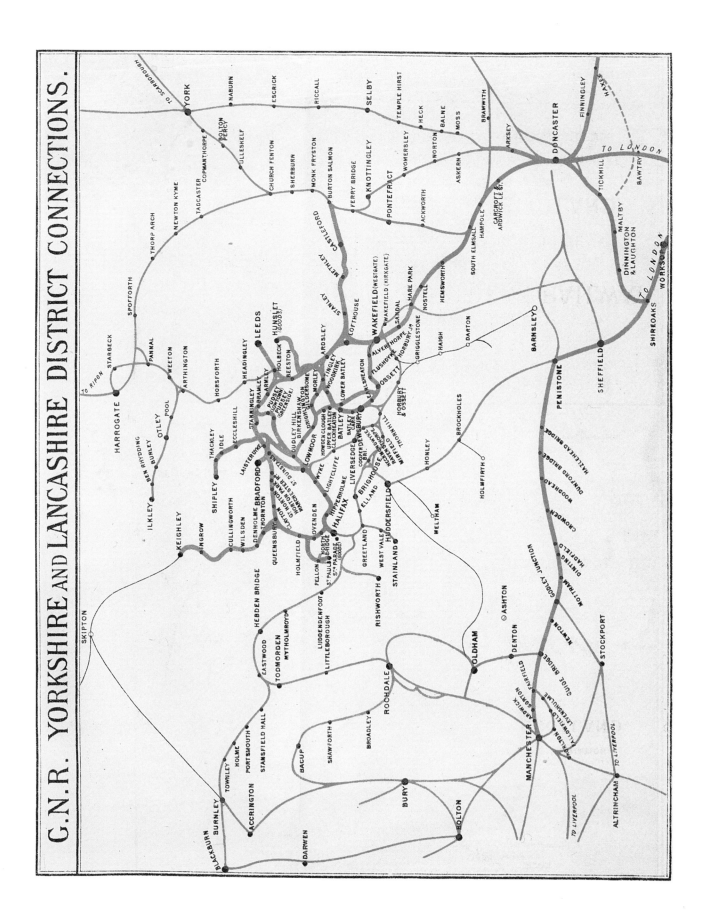

1st APRIL to 30th JUNE, 1913.

NORTH EASTERN
RAILWAY
TIME TABLES

Gratuitous.

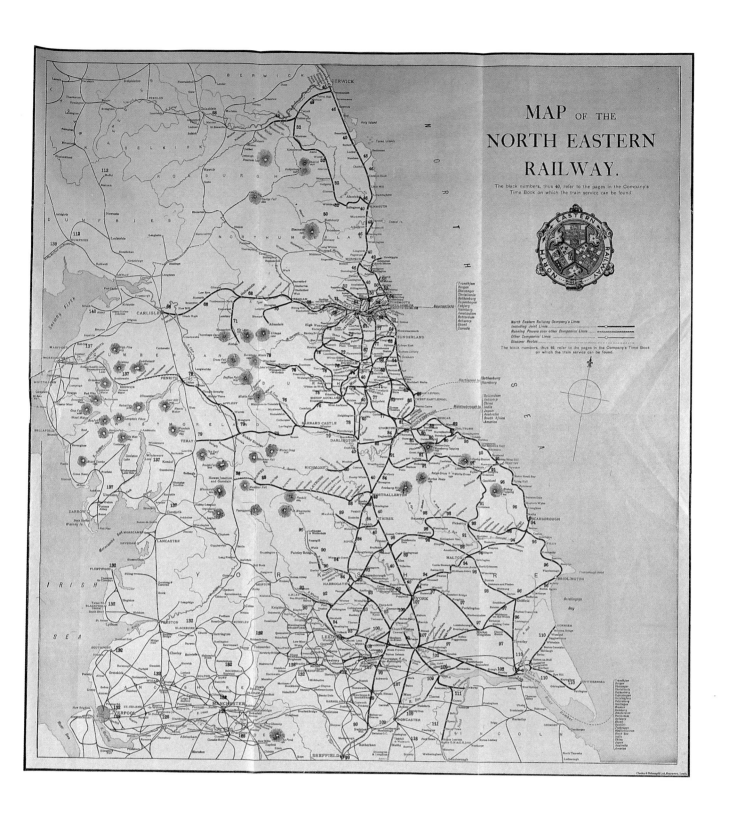

MAP OF THE NORTH EASTERN RAILWAY.

The black numbers, thus 40, refer to the pages in the Company's Time Book on which the train service can be found.

North Eastern Railway Company's Lines
including Joint Lines
Running Powers over other Companies' Lines
Other Companies' Lines
Steamer Routes

The black numbers, thus 40, refer to the pages in the Company's Time Book on which the train service can be found.

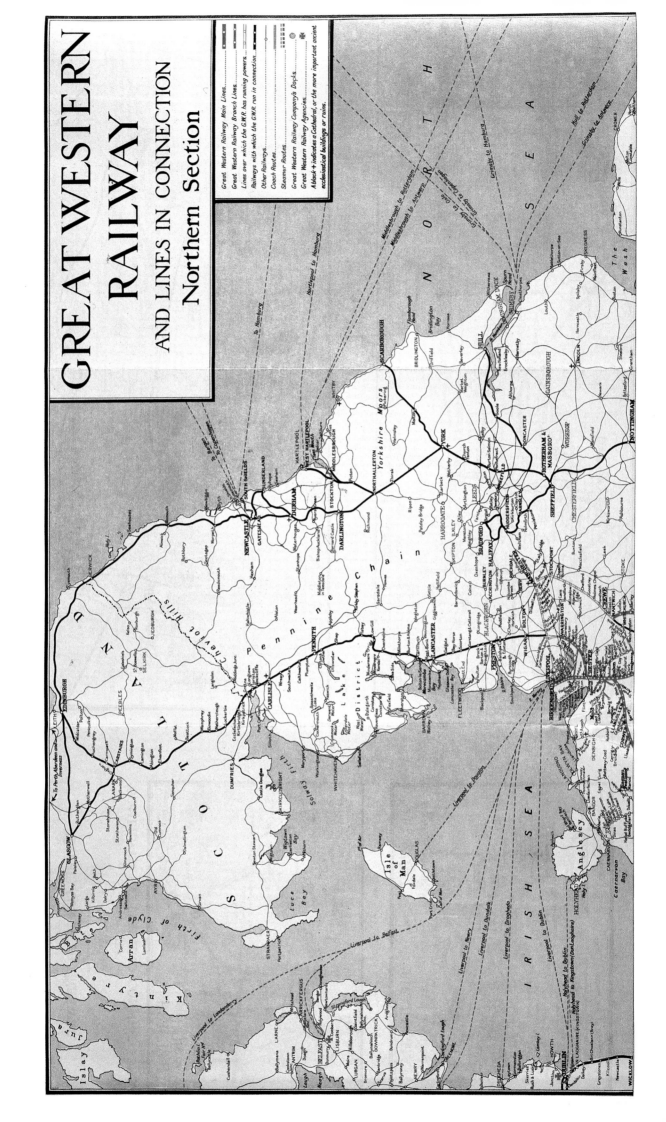

GREAT WESTERN RAILWAY

AND LINES IN CONNECTION
Northern Section

Great Western Railway Main Lines............
Great Western Railway Branch Lines.........
Lines over which the G.W.R. has running powers...
Railways with which the GWR run in connection...
Other Railways.....................
Coach Routes......................
Steamer Routes....................
Great Western Railway Company's Docks.....
Great Western Railway Agencies.............
A black + indicates a Cathedral, or the more important ancient
ecclesiastical buildings or ruins.

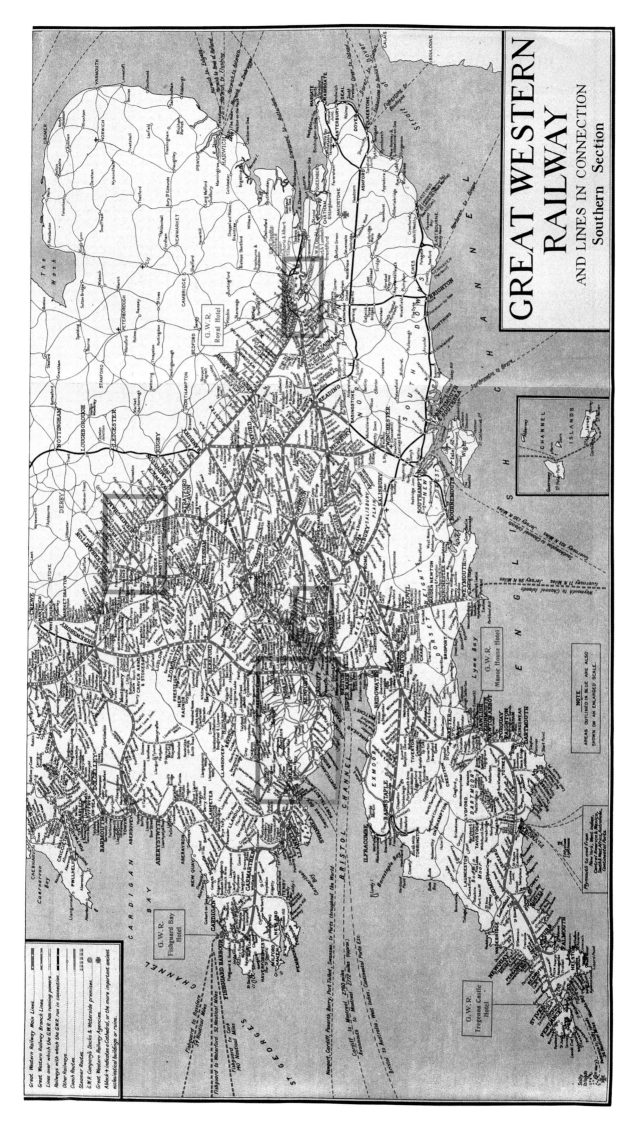

GREAT WESTERN RAILWAY
AND LINES IN CONNECTION
Southern Section

THE CAMBRIAN RAILWAYS
AND COMMUNICATIONS.

Cambrian Railways and Lines run over Coloured

Route of Through Carriages over other Lines ------

Terminal Stations from and to which Through
  Carriages run are shewn thus :— EUSTON STN.

For Train Service from and to all the Principal
Stations see Index, page 3, of the Company's
Penny Time Book.

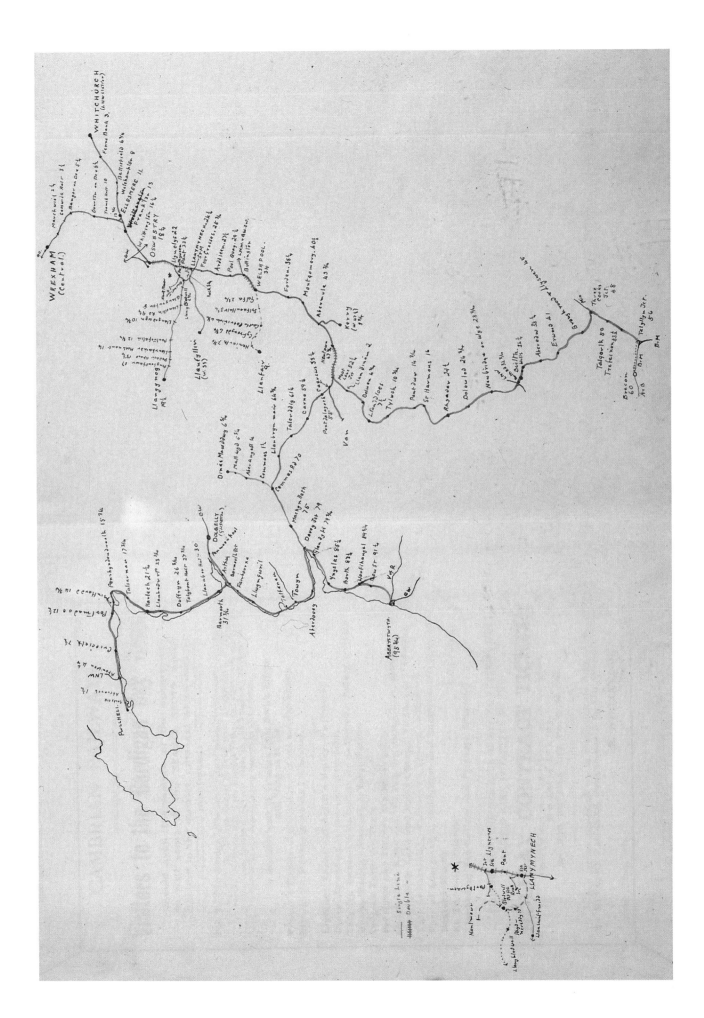

39

THE CALEDONIAN RAILWAY AND ITS CONNECTIONS IN SCOTLAND

PRINCES ST. STATION HOTEL, EDINBURGH.

CENTRAL STATION HOTEL, GLASGOW.

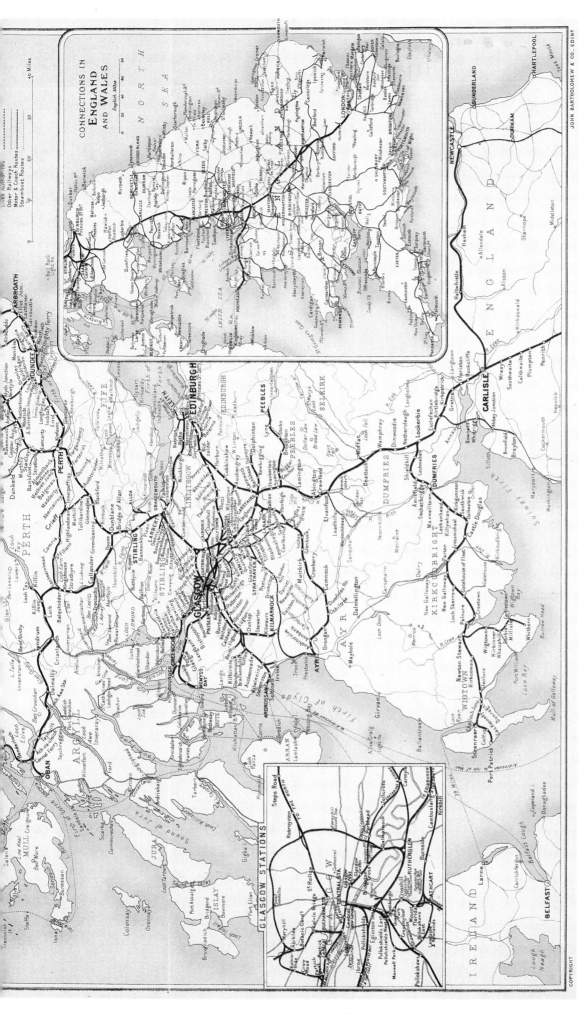

41

THE
CALEDONIAN RAILWAY

TIME TABLES

6th FEBRUARY, 1922, and until Further Notice

DONALD A MATHESON
GENERAL MANAGER

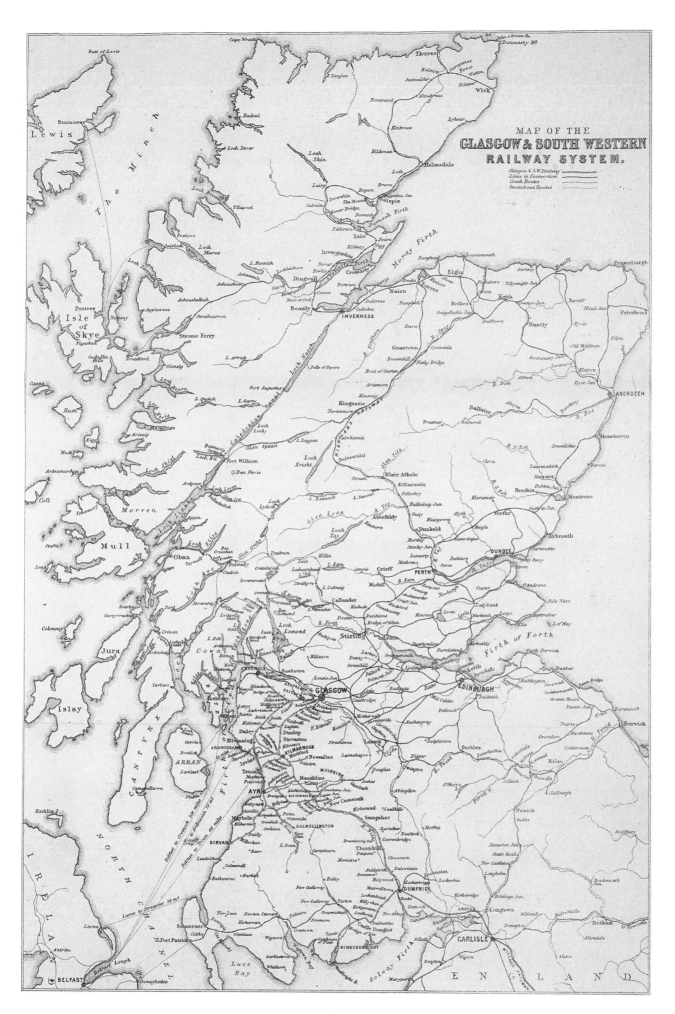

MAP OF THE
GLASGOW & SOUTH WESTERN
RAILWAY SYSTEM.

Glasgow S.S.W. Railway
Lines in Connection
Coach Routes
Steamboat Routes

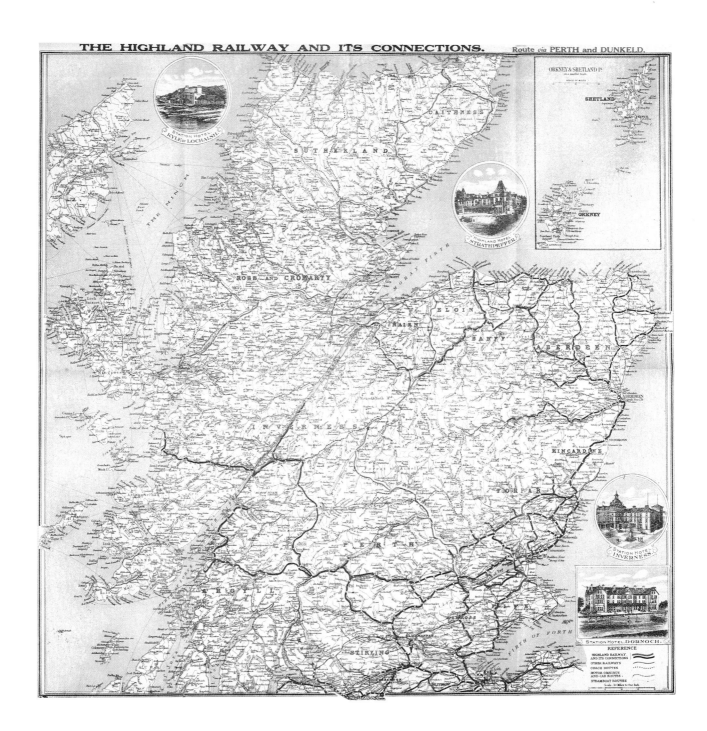

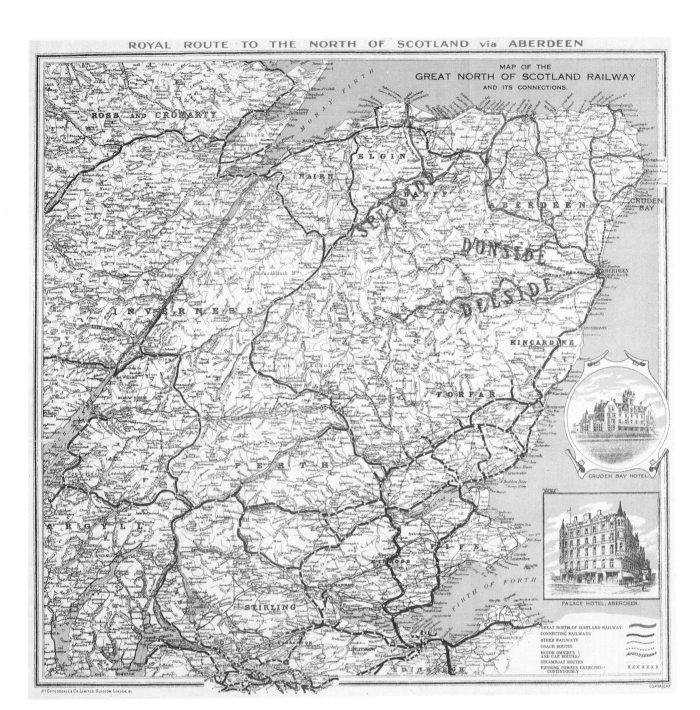

MAP OF THE
GREAT NORTH OF SCOTLAND RAILWAY
AND ITS CONNECTIONS.

CRUDEN BAY HOTEL.

PALACE HOTEL, ABERDEEN.

GREAT NORTH OF SCOTLAND RAILWAY
CONNECTING RAILWAYS
OTHER RAILWAYS
COACH ROUTES
MOTOR OMNIBUS
AND CAR ROUTES
STEAMBOAT ROUTES
RUNNING POWERS EXERCISED
CONTINUOUSLY

COPYRIGHT

45

SOUTHERN RAILWAY

STANDARD TIME TABLES

Including
SUMMARIES OF PRINCIPAL EXPRESSES, CHEAP FARES, CONTINENTAL AND AIR SERVICES
(SEE COLOURED INSETS)

SEPTEMBER 28TH 1936 UNTIL FURTHER NOTICE

SEE SPECIAL NOTE ON INSIDE FRONT COVER

PRICE 6D

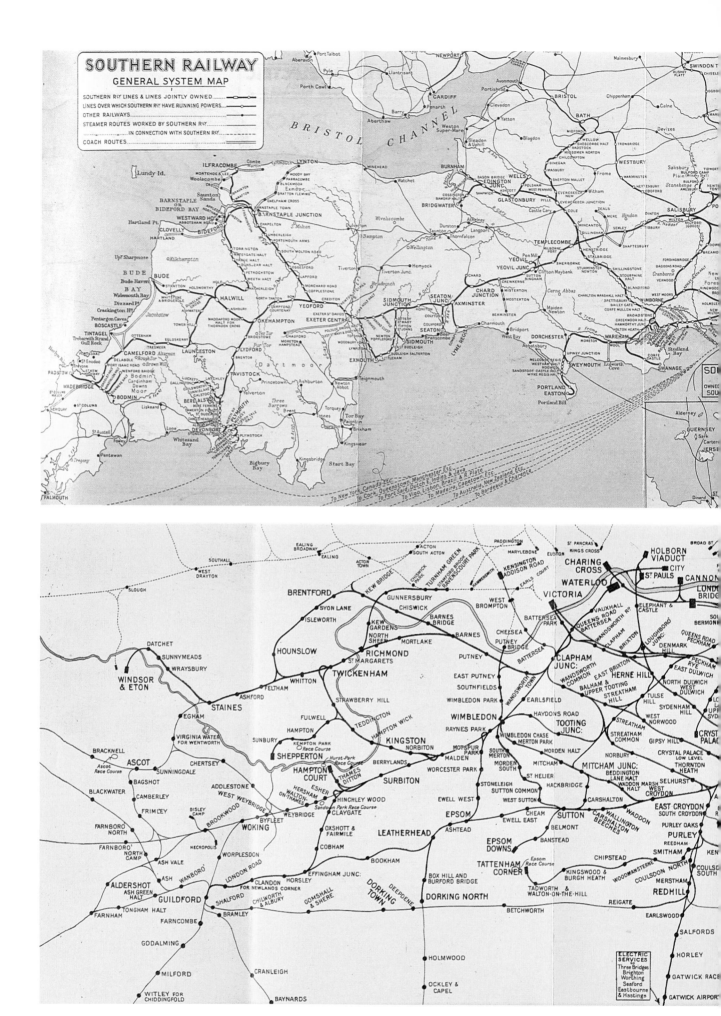

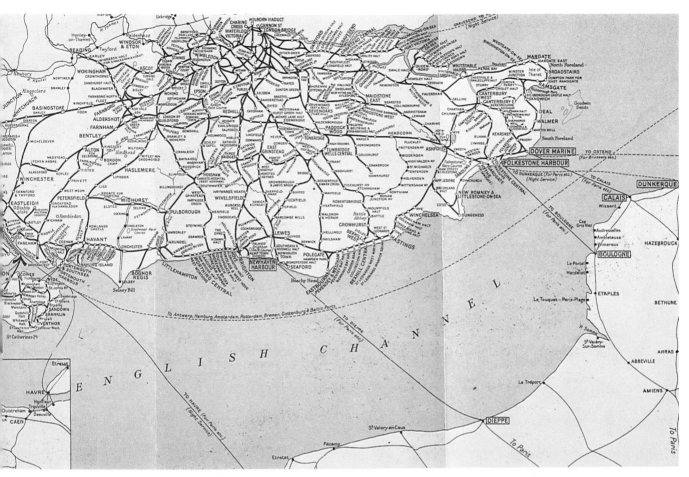

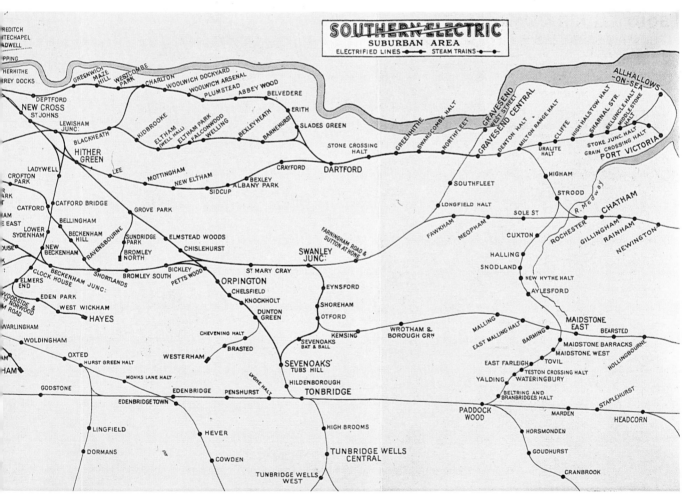

49

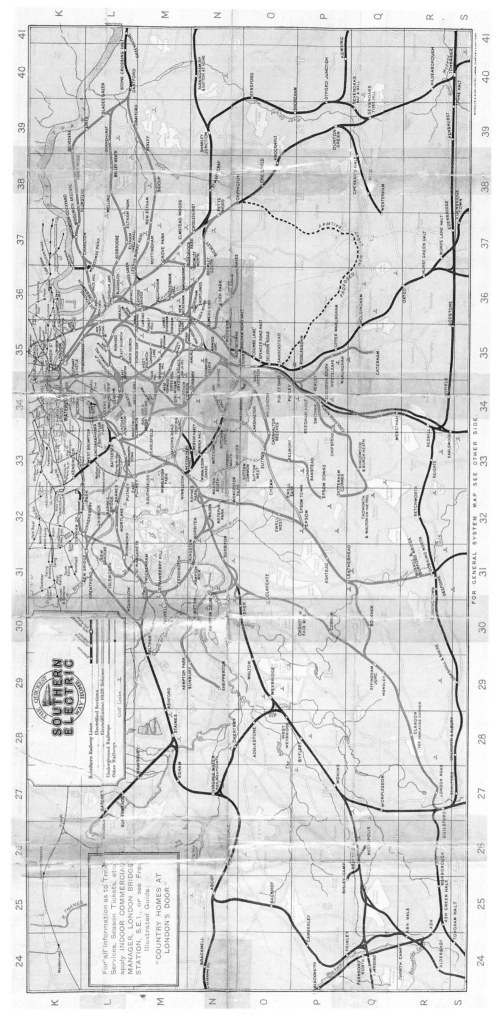

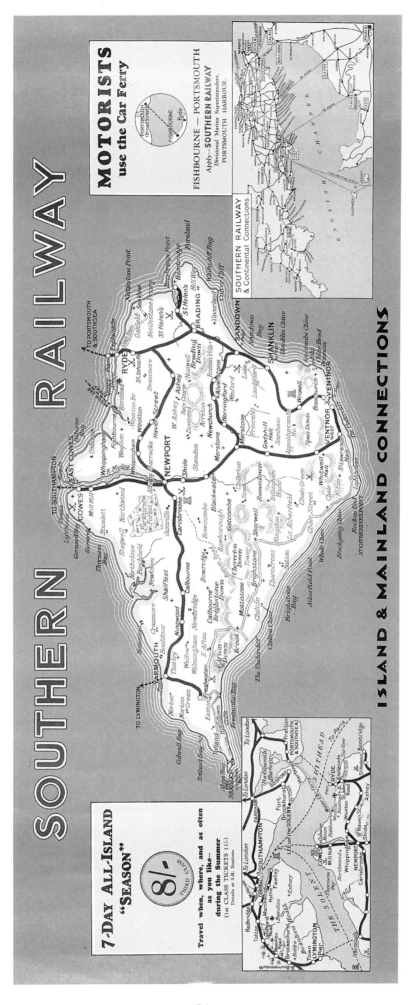

SOUTHERN RAILWAY

ISLAND & MAINLAND CONNECTIONS

7-DAY ALL-ISLAND "SEASON"

8/- THIRD CLASS

Travel when, where, and as often as you like—during the Summer

(1st CLASS TICKETS 11/-)
Details at S.R. Stations

MOTORISTS use the Car Ferry

FISHBOURNE — PORTSMOUTH

Apply—SOUTHERN RAILWAY
Divisional Marine Superintendent,
PORTSMOUTH HARBOUR.

SOUTHERN RAILWAY
& Continental Connections.

51

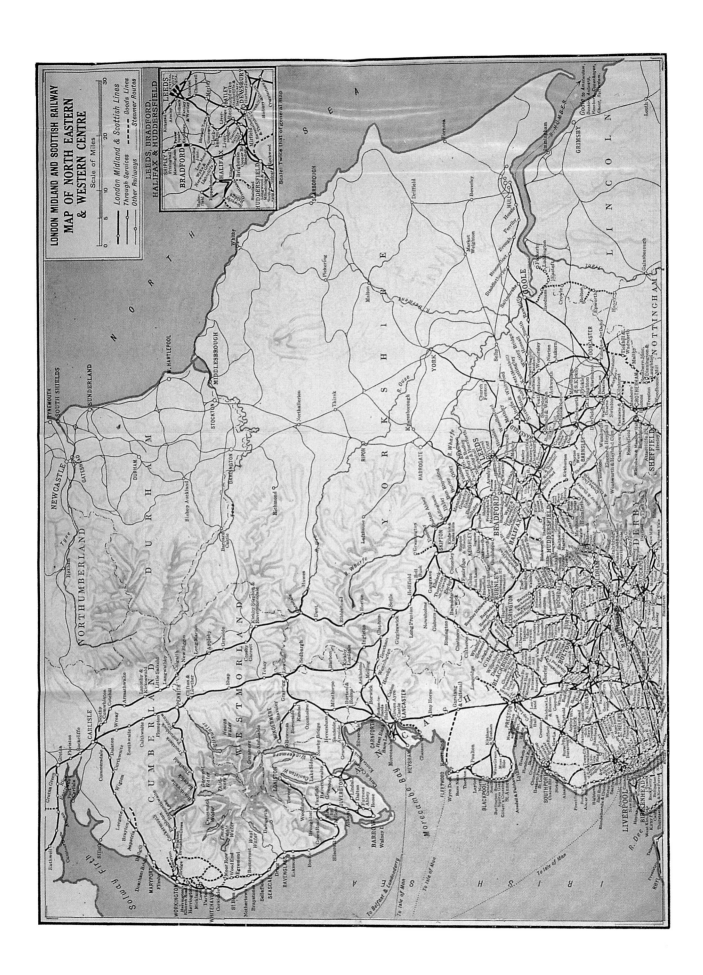

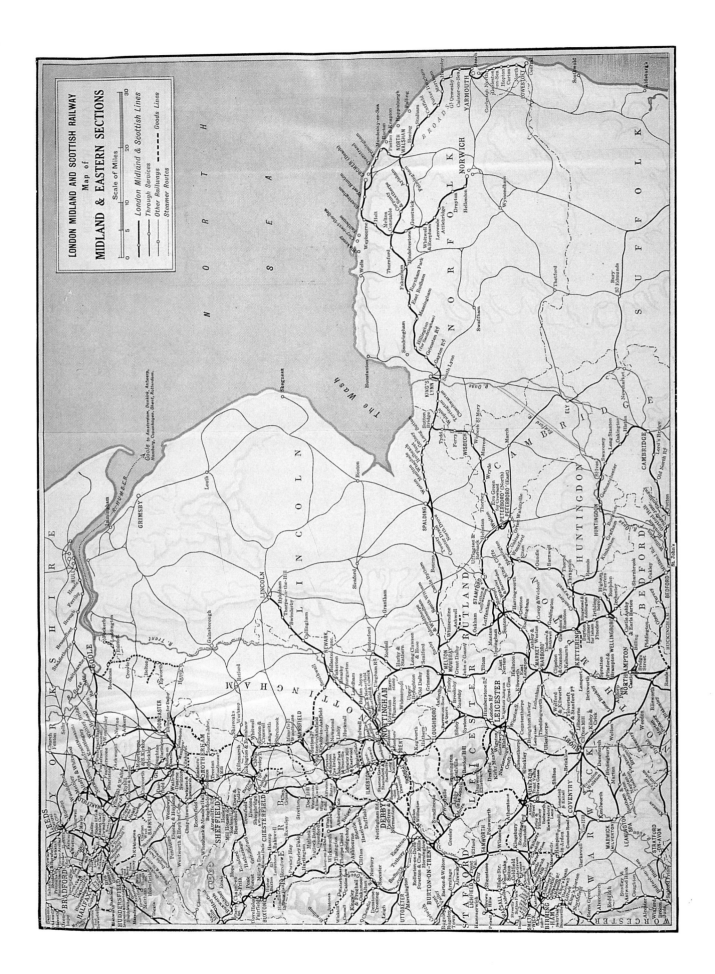

LONDON MIDLAND AND SCOTTISH RAILWAY
Map of
LAKE DISTRICT & LANCASHIRE

Scale of Miles
0   5   10   20   30

London Midland and Scottish Lines
Goods Lines
Other Railways
Steamer Routes

NORTH OF IRELAND. L.M.S. LINES & CONNECTING COACH ROUTES

LIVERPOOL & MANCHESTER

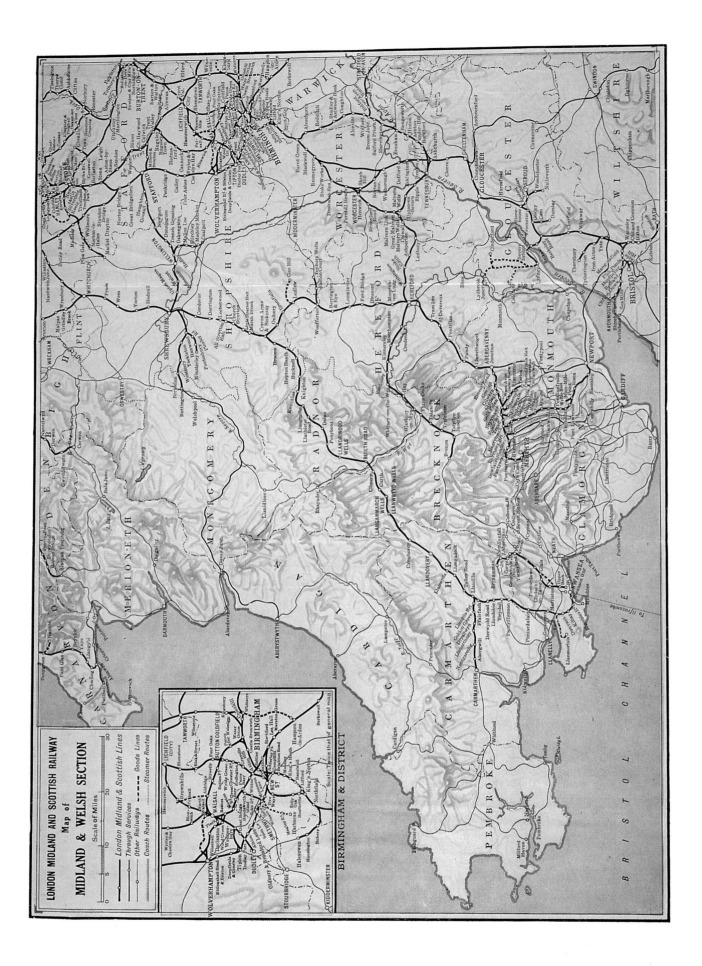

LONDON MIDLAND AND SCOTTISH RAILWAY
Map of
MIDLAND & WELSH SECTION

Scale of Miles

London Midland & Scottish Lines
Through Services
Other Railways
Goods Lines
Coach Routes
Steamer Routes

BIRMINGHAM & DISTRICT

Scale: Twice that of general map.

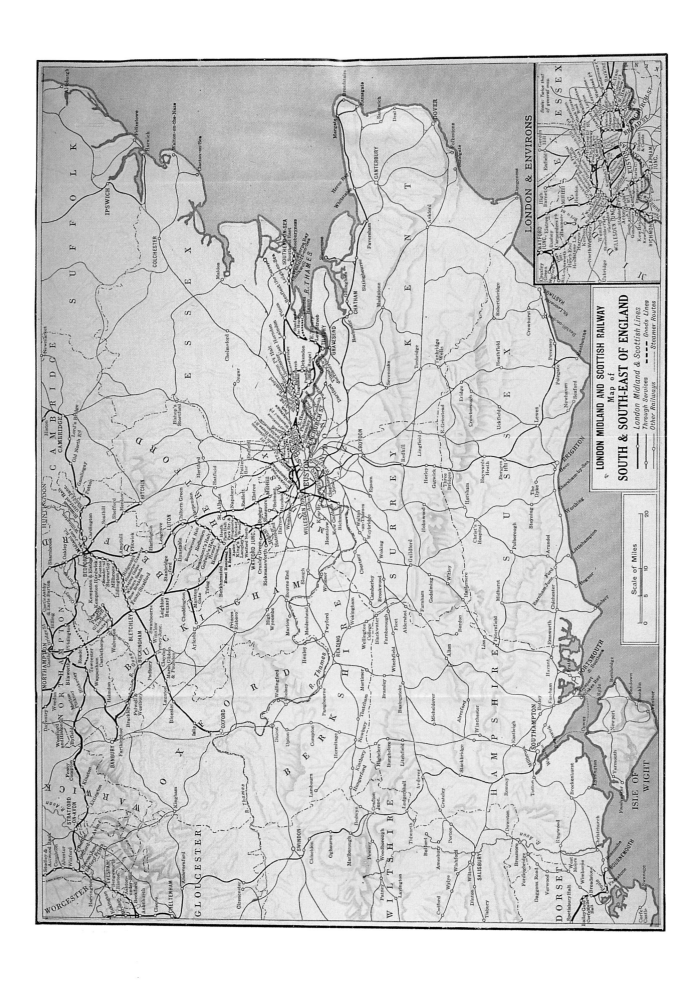

LONDON MIDLAND AND SCOTTISH RAILWAY
Map of
SOUTH & SOUTH-EAST OF ENGLAND

LONDON & ENVIRONS

London Midland & Scottish Lines
Through Services
Other Railways
Bonds Lines
Steamer Routes

Scale of Miles
0   5   10   20

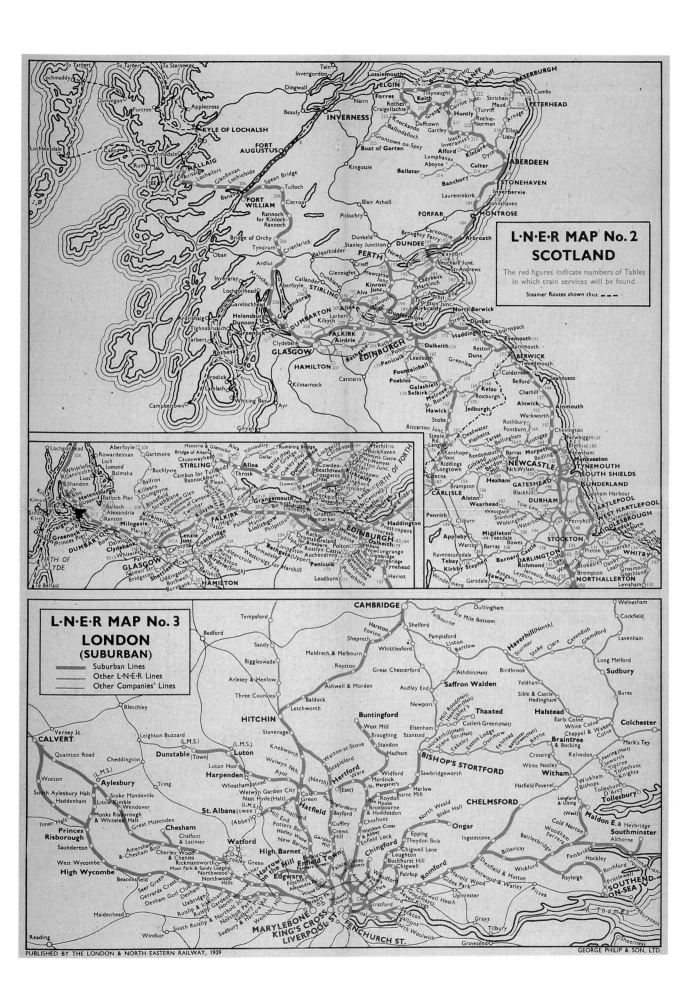

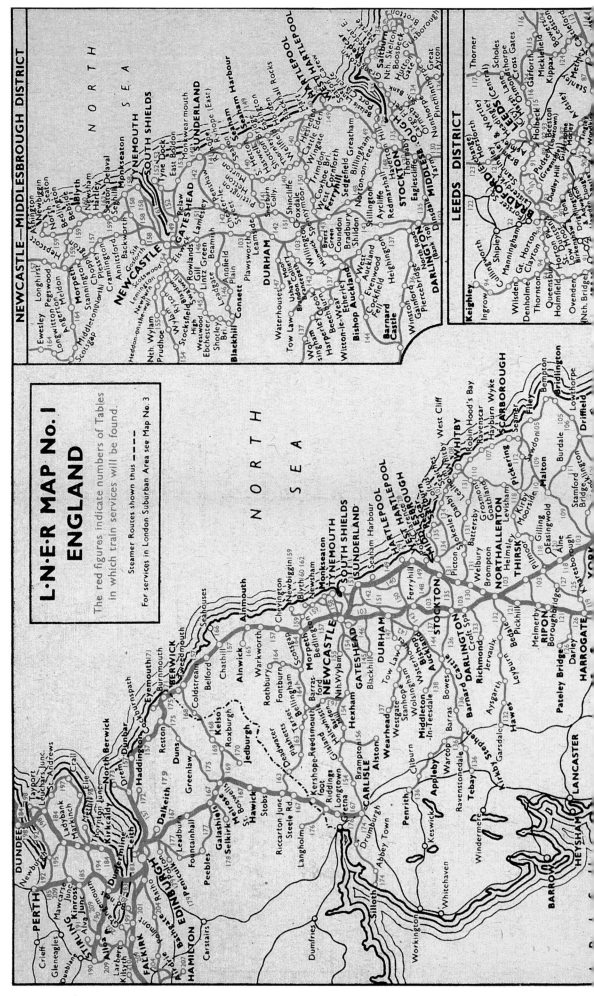

LEEDS DISTRICT

L·N·E·R MAP No. 1
ENGLAND

The red figures indicate numbers of Tables in which train services will be found.

Steamer Routes shown thus ----

For services in London Suburban Area see Map No. 3

NORTH SEA

58

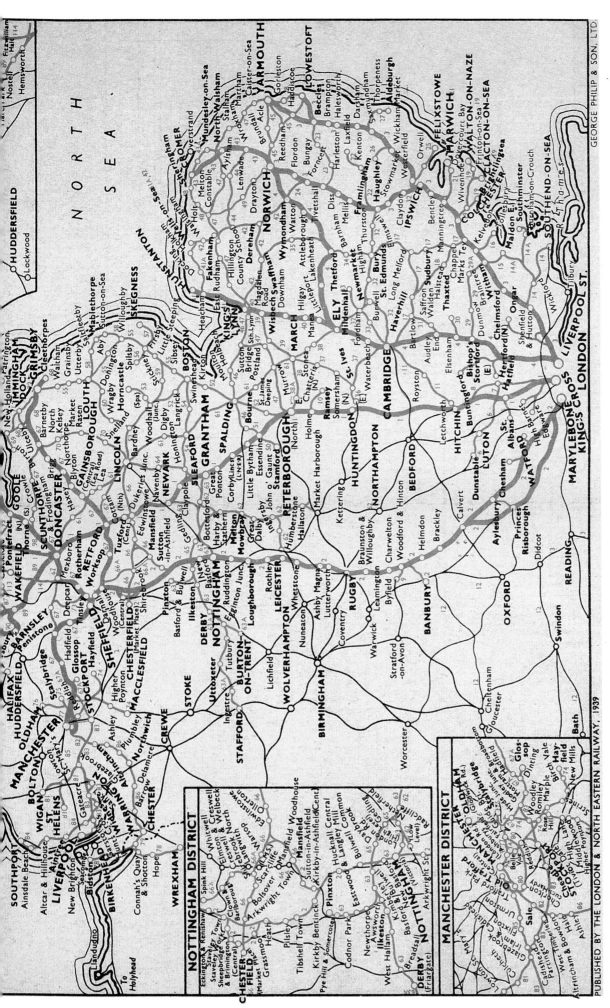

PUBLISHED BY THE LONDON & NORTH EASTERN RAILWAY, 1939

GEORGE PHILIP & SON, LTD.

60

GROSVENOR HOTEL

VICTORIA STATION, BELGRAVIA, S.W.

The most convenient stopping place for Travellers to and from the Continent. One of the finest and most comfortable hotels in Europe. Near fashionable centres, best shopping district and theatres, and central for chief places of interest.

Single and Double Bedrooms from **5/-** and **9/-** per day, including Attendance and Light.

FINE GRILL ROOM, DINING ROOM, AND TEA ROOM ON STATION PLATFORM.

LUNCHEON, 12 to 3, **2/-**.   DINNER, 6 to 9, **3/-**.

Also Service à la Carte.

Telegraphic Address:—Grosvenor Hotel, London.   Telephone No.:—9661, Gerrard.

Under the
Management of **THE GORDON HOTELS, LTD.**

LONDON

HOTEL GREAT CENTRAL

Favourite Rendezvous for Travellers from the North

Close to the Terminus of the Great Central Railway, enjoying all the delightfully fresh air of the Regent's Park and adjacent heights, yet within a few minutes of the Marble Arch, Hyde Park, and other fashionable centres of the West End as well as Club and Medico Land, the Art World, Lord's Cricket Ground, and Madame Tussaud's

LIGHT   AIR   HEALTH   COMFORT

INCLUSIVE TERMS : from 15/- per Day

For a stay of not less than One Week

Designed to afford all the comfort and refinement of a well-ordered mansion without its attendant anxiety, and also without extravagant outlay. The spacious central courtyard secures grateful seclusion to arriving and departing guests, gives light and air to every room, while the terraced footway surrounding it provides a pleasant promenade

ORCHESTRA IN WINTER GARDEN
MAGNIFICENT PUBLIC-ROOMS   ELEGANT PRIVATE SUITES
BEDROOMS WITH BATHS ATTACHED
RESTAURANT   RENOWNED CUISINE

DECORATION AND FURNISHING BY MAPLE

BROCHURE ON APPLICATION TO MANAGER

Telegrams:—" Centellare, London"   G. SCHMEIDER

'A TEMPLE OF LUXURY'

With Tariff more moderate than any other Hotel of the same class in London.

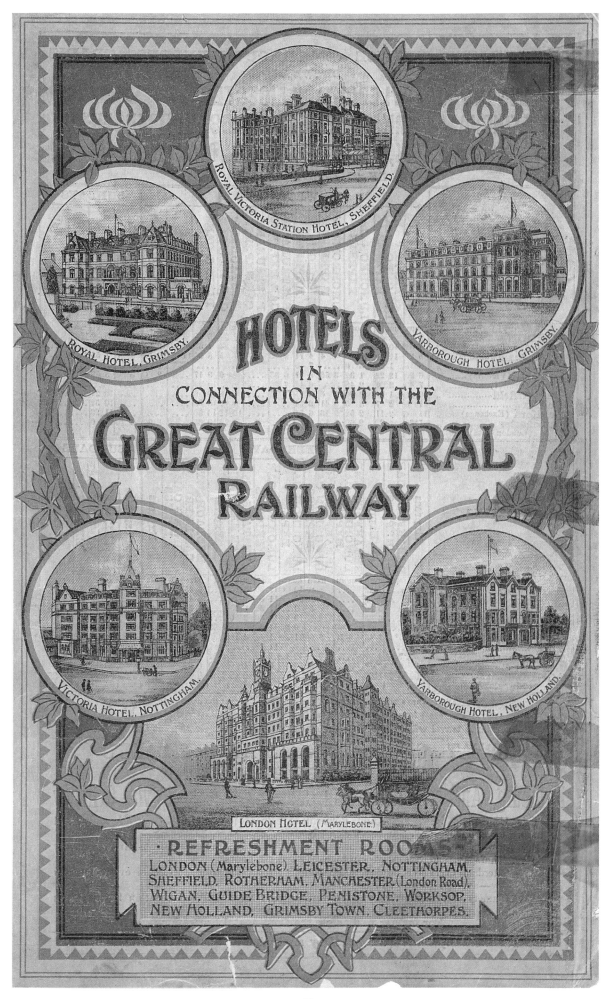

ROYAL VICTORIA STATION HOTEL, SHEFFIELD.

ROYAL HOTEL, GRIMSBY.

YARBOROUGH HOTEL, GRIMSBY.

VICTORIA HOTEL, NOTTINGHAM.

YARBOROUGH HOTEL, NEW HOLLAND.

LONDON HOTEL (MARYLEBONE.)

HOTELS
IN
CONNECTION WITH THE
GREAT CENTRAL
RAILWAY

REFRESHMENT ROOMS.
LONDON (Marylebone) LEICESTER, NOTTINGHAM,
SHEFFIELD, ROTHERHAM, MANCHESTER (London Road),
WIGAN, GUIDE BRIDGE, PENISTONE, WORKSOP,
NEW HOLLAND, GRIMSBY TOWN, CLEETHORPES.